Conversational Skills Ultimate Social Guide :The Art Of Socializing

Improve relationships, Enhance Conversation, and Become likeable

I0413994

Table of Contents

Introduction

I want to thank you for choosing this book, '*Conversational Skills Ultimate Social Skills: The Art of Socializing - Improve relationships, Enhance Conversation, and Become likeable.*'

Human beings thrive on social interaction and cannot function at their full potential without it. Socializing is a skill often overlooked and, unfortunately, one that becomes dull, unsharpened and simply deteriorates over time when left on the back burner. Perhaps humans have this false sense or notion that these skills come naturally and there is no need to look back on, refine and meticulously improve one's social skills, but this book, on the contrary, is here to show you the importance of fine-tuning your social abilities.

Whether you want to improve personal relationships, enhance small talk or network the right businesses or employers in pursuit of an opportunity, strong social skills are paramount. No civilization has flourished without paying attention to social communication, an important spoke in the wheel of socializing. History stands evidence to the fact that if social communication were not there, mankind would have perished long ago. The importance of socializing has been long underestimated in today's fast paced world. However, this book promises to accompany you on the journey of achieving a brag-worthy set of social skills that will go a long way toward making you a smarter, better and a more vital part of society.

Chapter 1: How to Become Likeable

Ever since we were kids, it has been taught to us that we need to be achievers. An achiever, through society's lens, is a person who has done well in life. Now the definition of having done well in life is relatively restricted in today's world. Society's expectations of you stop when you make a successful person out of who you are. In its eyes, when you stop depending on your parents, work a corporate job, acquire a property of your own and have kids, you are "settled" and "doing well." However, it forgets to emphasize a more important facet of human life which is socializing.

The last thing you want to be is in "your face" and obnoxious although society dictates you to be the epitome of this by being aggressive , spotlight stealing, and an attention seeker! On the contrary you need to be subtle, generous, kind and always offer to help when you can. Know your cues, allow other recipients to talk and input their opinions or perspective. This is key and crucial because you are creating an inclusive environment which makes people feel welcome and gives a sense of belonging.

The truth is people want to be acknowledged and heard as this is the ultimate validation and greatest sense of belonging. People want to be involved in the engagement process, affirmed and perceived as "important".

We are expected to win big in life. We are hounded when we fail to achieve success and compete with our fellow racers, and we are shunned when we give up on the race itself. Society does not allow us space and time to catch our breath while it pushes us to reach heights, the heights of which have been conventionally set. There is always a constant burden on our shoulders to be competitive and remain in the spotlight for the world to see how good we are while, in actuality, we may be anywhere ranging from below average to decent.

Subtlety

One of the best traits for a public speaker is subtlety. Do not always put things in peoples' faces. Be indirect and less straight. Let people put in the effort to figure out what you are trying to say. The best advantage of this is that when you hand your information over to people on a plate, they find it ordinary. However, when you create a puzzle that needs to be figured out before the information can be received, it makes the procedure interesting and the end result is all the more rewarding. Besides that, being subtle also saves you from the embarrassment of coming across as rude and imposing. You want to obviously finish painting the picture of a given topic your discussing and don't leave the crowd hanging or guessing, but the point here is be subtle and slowly put the pieces together.

Generosity

Honestly, if you are not a good human being, the chances of people liking you start from negative instead of zero. Being generous is not something that everyone is into. You have to have a good heart first. In order to do so, you must get rid of everything evil from your mind. Be selfless for a start. When you are selfless, you tend to see all the ways you can be productive and helpful towards others. Thinking of others before yourself is the first step to being generous. It needs to be mentioned that being generous does not equate to being a pushover. Know your boundaries and be willing to help people when they are in need of it. Being a selfless philanthropist will only lead to you being fooled in this cruel world. Life or the "universe" has a way of paying you back depending on what kind of attitude and actions you put forth. "What comes around goes around", right?

Kindness

It may sound like a broken record, but being a good human being also includes being kind towards your fellow man. You could be working in an office or just hanging out at the local bar when you create an impression that you are kind. People tend to have a lasting impression when you are kind. In this world of cutthroat competition, it is challenging to find people who are kind. You may get talented, sarcastic, funny and highly knowledgeable people, but kind people are rare to come by. Hence, to boost up your likeability, you must try to incorporate the quality of kindness into your personality. It is not an overnight process that will just happen at the snap of your fingers. You need to be continuously developing the trait.

Offer to pay for someone's meal, go the extra mile and do favors without expecting anything in return. Again, this does not equate to being a pushover, set your boundaries and know your limits, and know especially when to say, NO.

It's not rocket science to become a likable person. As mentioned before, it is not an over-night process either. It takes time and is dependent upon how fast you are willing to bring changes into your life. Help others and act kindly and it will improve your chances of being liked by others.

The Art of Story Telling

Storytelling is a dying art

Gone are the days when grandparents would sit you down and tell you about knights and mighty beasts. With the advent of technology, no one is willing to even pick up a book to read. There are Kindles and other devices that provide you with books online. The charm of storytelling has been dying for a while now. It is therefore not a surprise that no one is enthusiastic about being a good storyteller anymore. However, if you want to become likable, you must know how to be a good storyteller.

Measure The Mood:

You can't just grab a mic, hog the limelight and start talking. Before being the center of attraction, you must have a fair understanding of what mood the crowd is currently in. What sort of gathering is it? Is it a funeral or a hanging-out session with friends? It does not make sense to go on and start telling stories in a funeral. However, it does make sense if it's in a bar. Even then, a lot depends on the occasion and the general mood of the audience. If people are grieving, you can't tell them about that one time Aunt Marge farted when the guests arrived – unless it's relevant and lifts the mood of people present.

Pick a Topic Wisely

Do not just randomly pick a topic and rant about it with no regard of who's your audience. Just because you feel strongly about a particular topic does not mean everyone else will too! Cater to the audience as if it were you sitting there. If a random person were to talk about this topic, what would you think? Would you judge the topic then? Or would it have been relatable to you?

Be Humorous:

What is life without some humor? When you are humorous, people will find the most uncomfortable of topics bearable and funny. The element of humor is essential when it comes to public conversation. There may be some topics that are bland and lack any taste, but when you incorporate the much-needed ingredient of humor in them, they tend to get exciting and fun for listeners. For all you know, you could inspire people to go back home and research on topics they earlier found annoying.

A good storyteller needs not be a huge public figure. He could be anyone who likes to convey a good story to others. If he makes the public listen to him by constructing or narrating story, he is bound to enhance the chances of him being likable.

Humor is an element used by a lot of famous public/motivational speakers. Why? Simply because they're leveraging the body's inherent biochemistry, when we laugh this helps regulate the "feel good hormone" dopamine. The old adage proves to be true " laughter is good medicine for the heart", and laughter enables you to become a more likeable person because people will associate "feeling good" with you. A lot of university professors use this type of technique to stand out from the crowd and to give students a memorable   experience.

Chapter 2: Know Your Cues

When you have gone ahead and started talking publicly, you need to keep in mind a crucial aspect of public speaking; fishing for cues. Cues are such hints that let you know how your audience is responding to your words. Getting to know the cues provided by the audience can go a long way towards being a successful public speaker and ultimately a likable person. You must read and gauge your audience.

Be Observant

While talking, you must not lose focus on what is happening around you. Is the waiter shuffling around too much? If yes, that could be because people are busy ordering food, which could be a possible indication of people starting to lose interest in what you have to say. You can also look out for direct indications like people's facial expressions. Is the old man sitting at the far end of the room sniggering too much? Is the young crowd starting to get uneasy? Look around, and you will find their parents. Maybe it's a cue for you to stop talking about uncomfortable taboo topics such as sex. You need to be a thoroughly observant person to gauge the live reactions of people listening to you and act accordingly.

Other Conversation

You get to know a lot about the crowd by simply listening to their conversation. You do not have to eavesdrop or anything like that. Just be an onlooker. Join in the conversation if you must and contribute a little before going mute. When you listen to others' conversations, it gives you a rough idea about what the crowd likes, dislikes, has a strong opinion about and what to avoid completely. That helps you to be able to fit in.

Take Notes

Do not just be a mute observer. Learn lessons from your observations. Create a mental notepad where you write down your observations, and your inferences are hence drawn from them. It is not enough for you to just see what's happening unless you convert your observations into inferences. You must mentally make notes of all that you learned in the last five minutes of observing a conversation.

Outcomes

Everything that you say has an impact. You may feel like people do not feel anything about what you just said, but they do. Once you have successfully delivered a sentence, it reaches peoples' minds, gets through their conversion processor and leaves behind an impact on their minds. When you choose to say something controversial, the impact tends to be bigger and more shocking. Naturally when you say something ordinary people react, but it's not shown on their faces due to the low intensity of the "shock value" attached to the ordinary thing that was just said.

Therefore, be observant and cognizant of the power of your messages. Weigh in the balance of how much impact, damage or perhaps inspiration will saying certain statements make? You decide and choose wisely.

Listening vs. Hearing

When you listen to people, you must pay close attention. Every little detail that they blurt out is being examined and studied. However, on the other hand, hearing is about being casual and nonchalant about paying attention when someone is talking. Hearing involves much less concentration than listening.

1. Listening is about letting others know that they are important. Taking time to process the messages that is being sent. On the other hand, when you "hear" people, you are sending the message that you do not find them important enough to cling on to every word that comes out of their mouths.
2. Listening enhances your knowledge as it makes you analyze everything that is being said. But when you hear things, you tend to be nonchalant about even the

most important topics. This way, you are likely to miss out on the knowledge that would have otherwise been a valuable addition to your mind.

3. When it comes to listening, most people tend to have a wholesome experience because they are involved in the entire conversation and not just parts of it. When you consume the whole conversation, you are likely to have a better understanding of the topic at hand. But when you are casual about it by hearing things, you receive only bits of the entire conversation and tend to reciprocate based on that little information you have. This can further leads to arguments, misunderstandings and disagreements. However, the person who had listened to everything that was being said is now enriched with a holistic understanding of the subject and can now take a neutral stance. A neutral person is less likely to be attacked than an individual who has picked a side. Always try to be a neutral person to be a likable figure. Even if you are choosing a side, be knowledgeable enough to know the other side's story.

4. People like to be reaffirmed that you are listening, and to do this simply by paraphrase the gist of their conversation. This has a positively reinforced impressionable effect on people's minds, as you show them **A)** you're listening and **B)** it shows your understanding their point of view.

To conclude this section I'd like to emphasize and reiterate some points. Becoming a "neutral party" in conversation is your best bet if you want to become likeable. Here is an example, in politics countries who tend to be neutral tend to have the least headaches, wars, and tensions among others.

Why is this? Simply because the ability to compromise, and not allowing differing ideologies to clash at the forefront, and in our case on a microcosmic scale, "different opinions". Now I am not suggesting to be fake or pretend to agree with something you may strongly dislike, however you can accept their differing point of views as opinions and not rebuke them, and still hold your morals, values, etc.

It's really about the delicacy in how you go about doing this. Accepting someone's opinion is not necessarily agreeing to what they are saying, however you are acknowledging their point of view although they may be erroneously wrong. You are showing respect to hear them out although you may not completely agree with them, and by doing this you have a neutral stance on any subject matter. It's not wrong to form your own opinion, but it's how you go executing your messages therein lies the problem. If you come off as a "know it all" you would most likely create a lot of enemies even if you are correct! But if you have a more subtle approach that respects the other person's differing opinion in conversation you should not have any problems.

Chapter 3: The Art of Conversation

Talking: This is how we know how to interact; how one human can express emotions to another, how you build deeper and wider social circles by the art of conversation. We use the word 'art' next to conversation because the best and smoothest conversations that ever take place happen with a certain artistic flow. They are the most enjoyable.

If there is a promotion you want to avail of or sell your product more successfully to the customer, talk through someone's miserable day, a smoother conversation will help you a lot. Often standing on a stage and performing also requires a certain back and forth interaction with the audience. These are the subtle qualities that will help you stand apart from the general crowd. You will soon be the person that people will seek out for advice. You will be the person they will prefer going to for buying that product and even the person whose concert tickets will sell extremely fast.

The most enjoyable conversations that happen don't have people wondering, "What am I going to say next?" Or "Is it my turn to talk?" The best conversations work on the principle of 'invite and inspire.' But before we discuss the concept, imagine working in a restaurant with your conversation partner.

Suppose you have to make a sandwich and there needs to be an equal contribution from both of you. You toast the bread and pass it to your partner. He adds lettuce and passes it back to you. You may add cheese next and slide it back. And that is how you make a perfect sandwich, by sliding it back and forth and contributing effort in equal amounts. That is how smooth conversations work. The toasted bread is the instigator of the conversation. It may be as subtle as "how are you?" Now if you want the sandwich to keep passing back and forth (the sandwich is a metaphor for the conversation), you should choose to reply with "I am fine. How are you?" as opposed to a mundane "I am fine, thank you." In the former scenario, you have passed on the conversation and also induced more discussion on the topic. Whereas in the latter scenario, the conversation was dropped midway, leaving the participants confused and uninterested.

This is the premise of 'invite and inspire. You want to further create conversation by establishing rapport with those whom you talk to, meaning getting to know them on a personal level.

Invite and Inspire

A metaphoric invitation in a conversation is when you say something that explicitly gets your partner to respond to you and knows when it is their turn to speak. This way the conversation doesn't lapse, and eventually, you can communicate your way. This should be the heart of your conversation but we will discuss that later. A good invitation is one that induces answers more than monosyllables and close-ended questions like 'yes' or 'no'. It is more thought provoking and requires your partner to provide you with more details. An example is "What did you do on the trip?" as opposed to "Did you have fun on the trip?" The latter undoubtedly will bid the other person to tell the full story, and create engagement whereas the former will only be replied with a mere yes or no.

You may choose to use exclamatory remarks to show that you are interested in what they have to say. An invitation in the form of "Oh that sounds interesting! Tell me more about it," will show that you are interested in the conversation, this will automatically make the other person enthusiastic about conversing with you and more willing to share details.

If you ask the other person for intimate conversations, you should be willing to share intimate details about yourself too. The level of intimacy will obviously depend on the kind of relationship you have with the other person. But remember, most questions boomerang. So it would be safe to remember that you will be expected to contribute details as much as you ask from the other person. However, as imploring as invitations are, seldom can you build an entire conversation on its basis. Too many invites in a single conversation can mar the natural flow and often can make it feel like an interview rather than an art-piece. Invitations are powerful tools, but they cannot be relied on one hundred percent to keep the conversation flow continual. And hence you incorporate inspiration into the conversation.

Inspiration is when you implore your partner to contribute to the conversation without explicitly asking them. But just like invitations, inspirations need to be deliberate so that you can successfully induce a smooth conversation. When the conversation is allowed to flow smoothly, your partner will liberally weigh into the conversation. They will be inspired by themselves to chime into the discussion with comfort and ease.

Consider the sandwich metaphor again. While passing the sandwich to your partner who is supposed to add jalapenos to the sandwich, he adds olives instead and then slides the sandwich back to you. Now, you know the standard recipe is to add mayonnaise on top of it, but you also know that ketchup will taste better with olives; so you add ketchup and pass it back. Here the person has deviated from the standard protocol, or the rigid structure/framework of invitation-response, and inspired you to be more creative. The conversation flow will thus not only be smoother but also genuine and more interesting - or the sandwich will taste better, metaphorically speaking.

An inspiring comment creates a welcome space for the other person. It will encourage them to interact but speaking won't be a compulsion. You can inspire in different ways. You can inspire them to share their curiosity. An example for this is if you say, "I think the new person in the office is great." But leave out the rest of the sentence ("Because he shared his lunch with me") hanging in the air. More often than not, it will spark the flame of curiosity and have the other person asking you the most obvious follow-up question ("Why?"). You can choose to inspire them to share their stories or thoughts on a particular topic, depending on the situation you find yourself in.

Inspiring is a powerful tool just like an invitation, but it also has the tendency of backfiring. It is not an exact rulebook, which you can follow, but it has the potency to be. Mentioning the brilliant concert you attended the previous night to a person who isn't interested in music might induce a blank stare instead of the expected curiosity. You have to follow your instinct as much as rely on the inspiration to share curiosity.

Combining the art to inspire and invite in harmony will result in the perfect conversation between two or more people. The invitation will add a structured and guided element to the conversation and inspiration will add interest and flexibility. Gliding between the art to invite and the art to inspire is the true art form that needs to be mastered to own the perfect set of social skills.

Following the above basic guidance, you can soon learn to live and cherish life, where you won't be feeling like a reject or standing alone. You will soon be rejoicing the social freedom that you have worked hard for and earned. You will find yourself in a society where people will adapt to hearing you patiently and mold themselves by being more accommodating to you and your desires. You'll soon be living in a world where love and acceptance will come your way as easily as success and power. Being a likable person is all about striking the right conversation and being able to carry it forward. You need to leave a lasting impression on the audience's mind.

Conversation Control Techniques

You need not be the only one talking in a conversation for you to take it to the desired direction. You could also be a mute spectator and still steer the conversation according to your whims. Here are some ways you could do the same.

Acknowledgment:

When you acknowledge a participant, you send across a message that even though you may or may not entirely agree with what is being said, you, at the very least, recognize the speaker's right to his view. Acknowledging a person's opinion will go a long way in making sure that he does not become hostile towards the conversation. He will reciprocate when it's your turn to speak. This is healthy for any conversation, especially sensitive or controversial ones.

Validation:

It is important to show that you are approving of someone's views. It is not enough that you mentally applaud what a person just said. It is important to voice out your approval towards their view. It also goes on to show how supportive people are about a conversation. On top of that it also reinforces the belief that they are a part of the group. This establishes and inclusive vibe and positive atmosphere.

Nudging:

If you see the conversation going off-track or completely missing the very point of the gathering, you can always take a stand and steer everyone into the right direction. You do not have to take over. All you have to do is subtly point out that the purpose of the gathering is different from what is being talked about. Conversations tend to go on tangents in the absence of a moderator. Play the role of a moderator for your group.

Controlling a conversation is not about being the only speaker. You could still have a say in how the conversation goes by being a passive participant who is occasionally contributing.

Chapter 4: Knowing Your Audience

A conversation is like the wind; it blows both ways. If you want to be a good conversationalist, you need to understand your audience first and master the essentials.

Ask the right questions. Questions that will probe the audience to open up and start talking. Once they start talking, listen carefully. For, in this lie your next question and the question after that. This is the phase that I call a miner. A miner is the one who mines necessary and relevant data and information about the entity, which is spilling its guts out for you.

This is very important because the rest of the conversation and your views, opinions and ideas will be customized accordingly, keeping in mind the likes, tastes and preferences of this particular audience, at least for as long as you are dealing with them.

If this demographic likes pizza, you will develop a new found interest for mozzarella, olives, Parmesan and all things Italian. If they like watching a game of baseball, you will talk about how similar it is to cricket, which happens to be your favorite sport. If they like adventure sports, you will talk about your fascination towards scuba divers and Para gliders. The trick is to be able to get inside their heads, crawl under their skin and understand them. Find out what they find interesting in you. I cannot stress enough about how important it is for you to relate to them and for them to relate to you. This shows that you care and are wholeheartedly invested and just as much interested in them.

There are no set rules to follow, no code of conducts, no maps that will teach you the best way to understand an audience, since it is not "one size fits all." For example, a girl you once dated liked pink; this does not necessarily imply that all girls you will ever date will like pink. Do not make such assumptions; you will end up making a fool of yourself in their eyes. If your friends like it when you make sexist remarks, this does not mean your mom will appreciate them as well.

The point that I am trying to make is learn to maneuver yourself according to the person sitting in front of you. Be your own critic even before anybody else gets to criticize you. Learn to adapt and do it as fast as possible because time and tide wait for no one.

Refrain from making strong political or religious statements against those political parties and religious institutions that your target audience is affiliated with or might feel strongly about. You do not want to start off on a wrong foot. Be very careful in this regard.

You have to discover your audience as you go, one step at a time. In the process of discovering them, you will discover certain aspects of yourself that you were earlier unaware of. You will learn many things about yourself that you did not know in the first place.

That is the beauty of knowing your audience, by means of a conversation that is centered on their likes and preferences. You lose yourself to only find a newer version of YOU, your own personality update, if you may.

Chapter 5: Enthusiasm & Positivity

How to encourage enthusiasm and positivity among your peers and friend circle:

First impression

The thing about clichés is that most clichés are true; the first impression is indeed your last impression. There is no debate to this; the naysayers can try something else and fail gloriously. You only get one opportunity to make a lasting impression, grab it before it is too late and make it count.

- ➤ Smile as often as possible; this will make you likable, charming and approachable. Hold eye contact in a conversation, be steady and subtle, this radiates an aura of unflinching confidence. Just don't start a staring competition. You don't want to come off as a psycho.
- ➤ Try to greet people with a firm handshake; the firmer the better, just don't fracture their arm. This is an old army tactic that is common among men of service. A firm handshake paints you as an individual who is strong of character and morally sound.
- ➤ Remember to introduce yourself in a clear and concise manner. No one likes a sloppy mouth or someone who blabbers aimlessly.
- ➤ While having a conversation, stress on the positive aspect of all things and refrain from discussing the negative aspects. Cynicism is bad for a first conversation, save it for the drunken ramblings by the bar with your boys and girls.
- ➤ If you try to fake your interest in something or someone for that matter, it shows in one-way or another. Hence, try to put on display some genuine and sincere interests.

- ➢ Put forth questions that will get them talking; do not ask personal questions.
- ➢ We all want to be heard and listened to attentively, so do the same when someone else is talking to you in a conversation.
- ➢ Dress sense matters, believe me, this is the one thing that is going to put you in a box, help the person in front of you classify you better, and make sure that they think that you belong to a unique class of individuals.

If it's the first meeting and your nerves are all shaky. Do not get worked up, this is completely normal and natural. Chances are that the other person is just as nervous about the meeting as you are. Admit to your nervousness up front, this is an amazing icebreaker, and both of you may end up having a nice long chat regarding the same feeling of anxiousness. Obviously, this must be demonstrated in a cool, calm and collected manner, with an air of nonchalance; you do not want to give off the vibes of desperation!

Avoid topics that are taboo or might lead to an intense debate, where both of you are stuck on the opposing end of a spectrum. This may end up with the other person begging to differ and you remaining disagreeable, which is a disaster for a first conversation.

Being able to relate to the other person and inducing similar feelings from them is the key. Know when to talk and when to take the right pauses. Allow the other person to involve and immerse themselves into the conversation.

Body language is very crucial in such situations. Face them directly and do not keep your arms crossed. Crossed arms are signs of defensiveness. If you are defensive, it foreshadows your ingrained hostility towards them. It shows lack of confidence, which you are trying to masquerade desperately.

Take the liberty to be mildly flirtatious but do not overdo it. Do not be borderline sleazy. Laughing always helps, seemingly accidental body contact, like the touching of arms and hands or running your hands through your hair, etc. can make the conversation feel a little more personal and intimate. This will strengthen the bond between the both of you.

Self-awareness is critical if you wish to go far in life. It is just as important in this context. Notice the other person's body language in a conversation; study it and how it shifts accordingly. If the topic which is being discussed is running out of juice and no longer invokes the same enthusiasm and spirit, it's time you change the topic altogether. A change of pace is always welcome.

If they are still displaying an unfavorable or hostile body language, the meeting is not going as planned, try to recognize the problem and if you fail to do so, know when to make an exit. Do not overstay your welcome, know when the party is over, do not wait until they make you pick up the trash off the floor. Keep your dignity intact at any cost. This will keep the door open for future encounters.

Would you want to hangout with yourself?

There are two kinds of people. The people we want to hang out with and those who we wish to avoid at all possible cost. None of us would want to be the latter. Despite that, chances are, we might wind up being exactly that person if we are not careful enough.

I want you to quickly analyze and assess yourself and ask yourself a few important questions.

- ➤ Would I want to hang out with myself?
- ➤ Do I have anything to offer that other people will consider interesting?
- ➤ What are my strengths and weaknesses as a social creature?

Consider all the pros and cons and weigh them side-by-side. Once you are done introspecting yourself honestly, it's time you lose the dead weights and gain the necessary, helpful traits.

Accept people for who they are and not for someone you would want them to be. Expectations lead to disappointment. Every person you will ever come across is going to be original in his own right. Begin appreciating their individuality and point out the things that you like or admire about them, they will start doing the same with you.

They must not feel that you are judgmental in nature and are judging them in anyway, for being who they inherently are. You need to remember and accept the fact that every single person is unique in his/her way. There is no such thing as normal; in fact, it is abnormal to actually expect everyone to fit in your mold of normal.

Display your concern for them with a timely inquiry of them and their family's health and well being, this shows that you have invested yourself in wishing well for them. Surprise these people with random acts of kindness; this shows that you care for them.

If you are hanging out with other people besides them, try to introduce both parties and form a group that has similar likes, tastes and preferences. This is how you attract more admirers and gain more followers.

Do not exclude someone from plans that you are making if you consider them important in your life. Talk to everyone;

do not hold any prejudice against anybody. Nobody is beneath you or above you, treat everyone equally.

Smile as often as possible. Smiling is a way of welcoming people, as it is an indicator that you are joyful, happy, content with life and open for a conversation because you seem more approachable.

Your harmony with a person depends on how much you can relate with a specific person. At any given time, if you are unable to relate with an individual then just reassure them that you understand them because, at the end of the day, every person just wants to be understood and acknowledged.

Once you befriend someone, learn to be a consistent friend; do not abandon them in times of crises to only show up when the good times arrive. No one likes a deserter; no one likes a scum; do not be one of them. (that's what you call FAKE friends)

Be an honorable person. Know how to keep your word and promises. An honorable personality does not need to ask for respect, such people command respect among their peers naturally. People will trust you when you confide in them.

In conclusion, try to imagine the kind of person that you would like to befriend and hang out with and build yourself towards becoming that ideal person.

Chapter 6: Combining Friends

I would like to start this chapter with a sobering fact not everyone will like each other for different reason. It is impossible to expect everyone to get along with each other, and in this same manner you wouldn't combine every single friend on your social network platforms, ie FB, Instagram, etc together. Why? From personal experiences and stories I've heard I know this to be true and I'll explain why..

There is no exact science to it and it really depends on the people you come across ...For example, I don't ever mix friends with business (imagine mixing oil and water). Nor do I combine friends who like going on adventures and playing sports with friends who like to party. I strategically keep them separate for various reasons, and the main reason is not to create friction as you don't know how friend *A* will react to friend *B*. Also, conversational topics will be diametrically be different, some friends I can have in depth intellectual and philosophical conversations, and some I can only talk about relationships and more practical things. Do you see the vast differences?

It may not be a good idea to combine friends from different walks of your life. People tend to be different. It is more so when they belong to different aspects of your life. Try to keep your professional colleagues separated from your neighbors. People from a similar field tend to connect more within themselves.

If you are facing trouble to keep friends outside a circle, do the following:

1. Buy three notepads from the stationary store. Mark one "Professional," the next "Personal" and the other "Leisure." -The fact is we will have professional friends we make at work, personal and close friends, and friends whom we have more of a leisure friendship with.

2. In the "Professional" notepad, write down the names of all your workplace colleagues. Make sure you refer to your office diary so that you do not miss out on any names. This way, everyone who is professionally related to you will be covered on one notepad.

3. Similarly, write down the names of your closet friends and relatives (preferably bonded by blood or marriage) in the next notepad.

4. In the third notepad, write down the name of every such person who falls under either both or neither of the previous categories. These could include your neighbors, office workers who are also your friends, old friends you are no longer in touch with, school friends, graduation folks or any random friend you made in the past.

5. You can replicate the process in your phone as well. When you save someone's number, it gives you the option to put the person in a group. Often the options are Family, Friends, Office and the like.

The point I am trying to make is that you must be aware of the dangers of mixing your professional and personal lives. Human nature is volatile, subjective and unpredictable. People from different walks of life have differing views on common subjects like politics, religion and world peace. When a crowd starts including people with such varied and extreme opinions, things tend to go out of hands. Hence, a separation goes a long way in ensuring the lack of any social friction.

Chapter 7: Body Language

Body language is a broad set of behaviors that includes sign language, which is often misinterpreted for its parent source. Sign language follows a particular set of rules while body language is more diversified than that. Sign language is limited to gestures; mostly hand movements while body language consists of a variety of aspects like postures, expressions, distance and time intervals between speeches. Sign language points towards only one possible interpretation. Body language interpretations, on the other hand, could range on various ends of the conversation spectrum.

The complexity of understanding body language stems from the fact that different people behave differently. For some, a thumbs up might be a good sign of positivity while for others it might be too formal to the taste. While it is considered a good thing to use index fingers to point while giving directions in some parts of the world, showing the same in a conversation is considered rude in some other parts. Hence, the complexities related to body language reading are based on the diverse cultures and such aspects of humanity. This diversity could be of culture, region, values, religion, practices, customs or even a set of beliefs.

Body language refers to the accumulation of physical signs and gestures that reveal a person's intention or state of mind at a given point of time. Primary examples of such signs and gestures can be facial expressions, eye movements, postures and touches. These are, however, some of the most basic forms of body language. The depths of body language remain to be seen, which we will delve into in the later sections of this book.

Body language could manifest itself in a wide range of forms. The following are some of the commonly witnessed ones -

Body postures

A person's body postures say a lot about what he is feeling. One's emotions can be expressed in various ways, one of the most effective of them being body posture. How you talk, walk, sit and assume a particular physical position conveys a great deal about what's going on inside your mind.

Interpretation about body postures is made by taking into consideration a neutral scale. When a person is in frustration he would display aggressive body postures., he would display submissive When he is depressed or reluctance pronouncing body positions.

In a group discussion, the following positions mean the following implications:

➢ Sitting back in the chair: Understanding and ready to listen
➢ Leaning forward with palms joined: Eager to not just participate, but also expecting to see others do the same.
➢ Cross-armed sitting position: Not welcome to others' opinions and in a strong mood to disagree with views put forth by seemingly neutral speakers. Very skeptical.

In an interview, a candidate's behavioral pattern could be inferred from the following signs:

Folded hands could mean too staunch a stand and infirmity of opinions. A smiling face coupled with a straight posture commands discipline in an interview. Likewise, fumbling knees and nail biting habits could indicate nervousness and anxiety.

In a simple conversation, feet pointed towards the addressee means you want him to listen to you and any deviation would be noticed. Similarly, a listener's body language patterns; two feet in different directions or standing with the entire weight placed on one leg displays a more casual attitude and suggests impatience or nonchalance towards the ongoing conversation.

Gestures

Gestures are physical movements made by body parts like legs, fingers, hands or arms that indicate towards a particular intention or emotion. Gestures could be classified into voluntary gestures and involuntary gestures. A gesture can be expressed in various situations like an interview or a group conversation. For example, sitting or standing with crossed arms is a negative gesture, taken to meant unwelcome attitude of the doer. It often leads to the conclusion that whatever suggestion others will make will be unacceptable according to the gesture maker's standards. On the contrary, one arm crossed over another could point towards a person's uneasy feelings and also a particular shortage of confidence.

In general, hand gestures can be classified into three types:

Type I: Relaxed hands are often swinging in joy. Such hands tell us that the person owning them is a secured person who is more than satisfied with his state of existence. It may come coupled with self-assurance.

Type II: Clenched fists indicate towards the anger or frustration of a person. Needless to mention, the person is either in a state of extreme irritation or heightened anger.

Type III: Unsure hands. Unsure hands could be wringing hands, crossed hands, tapping hands, or hands performing any activity that seems out of the ordinary. They often imply anxiety and nervousness. Insecurity is another trait that unsure hands may point towards.

Fingers

Thumbs up sign indicating 'everything's under control' or everything being all right is not an uncommon sight. An index finger sliding through your neck is a sign of upcoming danger that may prove fatal. Thumbs down sign show defeat or a challenge to race as one passes slowing down cars through the highway. Fingers can produce some particular obscene and offensive signs. The middle finger is universally known to suggest just that. More than rudeness, it reaches vulgarity if literal translations were taken into account.

Certain cultures consider it offensive to point fingers towards a person. On the other hand, some other cultures encourage using the index finger to point towards someone. Gesture usage varies according to countries. Thumbs up is a sign related with normalcy in the West while in Islamic countries it is the equivalent of showing the middle finger.

A public speaker cannot escape the use of fingers during the inspiring speech. Due to countries like Germany and France having had a history of public speakers that went on to become fearsome dictators, such countries do not mind when fingers are invariably used to indicate feelings.

Facial Expressions

Facial expression is an important part of body language that is expressed through physical movements. An amalgamation of eyebrow shifting, cheek movements, lip fluttering and eyes is what facial expressions are all about. They help one put the finger on a rough emotion of the individual being studied. The subject's mood in terms of happiness, sadness, anger or depression can be measured using a thorough assessment of facial expressions. Shifty eye movements are indicative of guilt in criminal investigations. Similarly, psychiatrists who deal with convicts to extract confession helpful in the solving of a new crime try to focus on their eyebrow movements to determine whether they are telling the truth or not. A mere fluttering of eyelashes is seen as a seductive gesture in classic movies, but in the field of criminology, it's seen as an attempt to cover up one's ulterior motive. It's seen as a coping mechanism to deal with nervousness produced from too much of anxiety.

Certain scientific experiments relying on tabulation studies have concluded that facial expression is not only a sub-set of bodily expression but also an independent sub-set functioning simultaneously and independently. The assumed bodily expressions are often related to facial expressions. It could imply that our brains interpret our facial and bodily expressions in the same way. Participants in these experiments were seen as recognizing bodily expressions the same way they recognized facial expressions.

Importance of Body Language

Not every thought that crosses your mind gets the privilege to be projected outside of your minds. Due to this, there arise circumstances where too much of bottling up leads to unpleasant and undesirable situations.

Then there are times when being able to read a person becomes a necessity than a luxury. Like in the field of law and crime solving, it is important to know the intention of the accused. Lie detector tests are too technical to be solely relied upon for efficient results. Psychologists and face readers supplement the investigation process by providing a rough estimate of the person's guilt or innocence.

Overall, being able to read body language helps you not only know what's going on inside someone's head but also how to plan your line of action accordingly. You get to choose the best course of action or conversation based on what you interpret the other person is thinking. Being able to read people is a gift that can be developed and used to great extents.

Chapter 8: Dangers of Over-Thinking and How to Avoid Them

Our mind is a tapestry, which can set us free if used efficiently. It can also imprison us in a prison of our own making. A prison full of tiny little voices that can break you.

If you let that little voices overpower you, it will manipulate you and multiply into a deafening incoherence. The voice can plunge your psyche into utter chaos if you are not mindful enough.

We call it over thinking. Most of us have this horrible habit, and most of us are tired of feeling like a walking, talking, breathing, ticking time bombs, which can explode at any given moment.

We over think because we are terrified of failing. We imagine all possible outcomes to a given situation, our resultant actions and inaction to those possible outcomes and start getting worked up over the negative outcomes and overjoyed over the positive ones, without ever actually getting any tangible work done, in the first place.

The primary problem with over thinking is that it will constantly shift your attention from the present. We have to remember that only the present is real and we have to live in the moment, not in the future and not in the past.

Your thoughts and worries will only multiply if you feed them hence the only effective way not to feed them are by employing this simple mind technique:

- ➢ Close your eyes.
- ➢ Visualize a phone.
- ➢ Visualize your bothersome thoughts as power consuming applications left open on your smartphone.

- ➤ Now visualize swiping upwards and closing each application one by one.
- ➤ As you do that, you will feel a little relaxed.
- ➤ You will feel like you are getting rid of your thoughts, one after another.
- ➤ Now channelize your thoughts and energy into doing something productive which will keep your mind occupied.
- ➤ Do not allow bothersome thoughts to find their way back into your head and corner you into over thinking.

What we need to keep in mind is that we must own up our actions in the past, learn from our mistakes and not be bitter or regretful over them. Regrets will wreck havoc and turn your life upside down. Learn to derive simple pleasures out of life, begin by enjoying your work and pay attention to yourself, your health, your family and the things which matter. Occupy yourself with things that will make a difference in your life, and you will notice yourself become more focused with the passage of time.

How to seek clarification and avoid misunderstandings

Remember that communication is the key to all your problems and lack of communication is the root of all mishaps. Lack of communication causes misunderstanding and misunderstandings lead to a clouded understanding of the situation at hand, which in turn may lead to a misjudgment.

Investing some of your precious time in knowing people better, what walks of life they come from and what are their traits will pay off in the long run. This is applicable in personal relationships building and also just as applicable at the workplace. We must learn to explain better and express ourselves so that we may avoid any misunderstanding with another individual. This can be achieved by phrasing your words and sentences correctly while holding a conversation. Perhaps replacing words like "YOU" which is closely associated with blame depending on the situation of course.

Words are like bullets and mouth is a loaded gun. Do not be fickle and leave your remarks or compliments open for interpretation. When you are dealing with a person, who is not on good terms with you, utilizing this line of dialogue will result in further complications and eventual collapse of your relationship with the said person.

Some people are easily misunderstood because they might try to masquerade their sadness and misery with the materialistic attitude towards life, which might paint them in an obnoxious and unfavorable light.

Try to see through their facade, eliminate the smokes and mirrors, Try to decipher and decode their emotions and raw feelings, which lie buried underneath the rubble of stony eyed gazes and cold exterior, assess your option and act according to the situation.

Nothing is more invaluable as a friend, who understands us, fights for us, protects us and guides us in our time of trouble and need.

Your efforts will not be wasted, the goodwill that you reap, if you play your cards right, will take you a long way.

Never Assume

Let me tell you a small story. I had a friend who assumed that everybody was capable of being compassionate and kind. He assumed that everybody would treat you fairly and do right by you if you do right by them. Clearly, he was a naive young man, and that was about to change, I am not sure if for the better or for the worse. He was cheated on in my first serious relationship. He had invested a lot of time, love, effort and care into this relationship and by the end of it I was distraught, hopeless and heartbroken.

His juvenile anger forced him to make another assumption, which was that people are inherently selfish and seek only the things that suit their own interests. If given a chance, they will only hurt you because we humans are animals of violence and unrest. He was mentally in a very dark place and spiraling down much faster than he intended or assumed.

What followed was a series of bad life decisions that he would go on to regret for the rest of his life. He turned into a horrible villain of a person, the kind that would not want to associate myself with.

He hurt people who meant well and were kind to himself. Who only wanted the best for him and intended no harm. He was blinded to all that was good and beautiful in people because he had assumed that people were incapable of kindness. So when the good stuff came knocking at his doorstep, he turned a blind eye to it.

He was not able to stick around long enough in any serious relationship because he was always too afraid or terrified of being cheated on, so I either abandoned them before they dumped him or he cheated on them before they ever had the chance to be unfaithful with me. It was a different kind of hell, to be honest. I was living a lie, and I knew it.

You see? An assumption can wreak havoc in your life. So one fine day, he decided that he would let go of all my assumptions. After all, these were the shackles that he was chained to. This was the baggage that he had to get rid of. So he told himself that it was about time that he gave himself a much-needed shot at redemption and allowed life a second chance.

He told himself that he would try to trust people but keep an eye out for the phony ones. It's no use looking at life through rose-tinted glasses when you can't even spot the alarming red flags. There is good in people; that does not mean we assume that all people are capable of good.

There is a lot of bad in people, sinners and wrongdoers are commonplace, which does not mean that we will be only met with unkindness in life. On some days you will have the dark clouds hovering over your head, and on other days there will be sunshine. By the way that was a true story, and that happened to a close friend of mine.

 Moral of the story do not take things at face value, the woods may be green, deep and beautiful, but that does not mean that the beauty is devoid of dangers. Tread carefully in your path. Take necessary precautions, wear your heart on your sleeve but do not allow yourself to be venerable.

Assumption is an essential trait because it has helped Neanderthal survive through the evolution of mankind, but now we have to curb our instincts and make it more rationale in nature.

Do not be swayed by impulses, keep your head steady, calm and composed. Think umpteen number of times before you make an assumption or pass judgment. Even if you end up assuming one thing, be open minded to new developments.

If something contradicts your predetermined assumptions, do not be afraid to change them for the better; "For the better" being the key-phrase.

In conclusion, just remember that all of the life decisions are binary; it's either a yes or a no. So go ahead and think things through, just don't over think them through. Because even if you think once or a hundred times, the answer is either going to be a yes or a no. Live in the moment. Own up all your actions. Have no regrets and do not over think.

BONUS - Conversation Dynamics

Conversation is always changing   there is no script to conversation and this may be terrifying to some as the fear of the unknown can be quite overwhelming. I want to quote a famous saying by the world renowned martial artist Bruce Lee " Be like water.", and this is precisely how you must be. I'll elaborate, the fluid and dynamic nature of conversation is quite clear and you cannot always have a script ready to engage in conversation. All dialogues can change in the blink of an eye and are influenced by many factors and variables in life.

It is impossible to pinpoint the exact nature of a particular conversation, but you must learn how to roll with the punches and go with the flow. What does water do? In a river it continuously flows, and when obstacles such as large boulders is on its path, water's flow does not get disrupted. But in actual fact it just subtly passes by creating a new path, not forcing the boulder out of its way. But the flow of water simply is diverted into a new path subtly without any aggression or force.

Translate this into the real world, into a real conversation. You don't necessarily need to grab a conversation by the throat or by the horns as they say. But you can use "subtlety" as we previously discussed in this book to gain leverage and be in control. Not only does water flow, but it is clear and transparent. Being clear and transparent is a good way to keep dialogue going, showing people your good intentions will make you a more likeable person. Water is the source of life, without it we would die. In the same manner conversation is the key source to communication and learning how to master this art of socializing is how you can become an excellent conversationalist, build strong lasting relationships and impressions, business connections, network, public speaking, social butterfly, and just become a great friend. The skill of conversation overlaps into so much areas in our lives. Without good conversational skills our communication within our social surroundings would greatly suffer.

Conclusion

Humans are social creature, they must communicate and socialize in order to get their thoughts to circulate. Social skills are vital when it comes to human civilization, to not only survive, but also move forward. In this book, we walked through the various aspects of a conversation.

Socializing as a concept was analytically dissected, broken down and studied through various lenses. The idea of body language in the realm of socialization also featured towards the end.

I hope this book was an informative and enjoyable read for you.

If you enjoyed reading this book may I ask you leave a quality review on Amazon. Please see the link below..

Thank you!

Link: http://amzn.to/2trzV2P

Other recommended books written by *Jason Gale*

How To Analyze People Ultimate Guide

LINK: http://amzn.to/2srLLa8

P.S--Remember to check out the last page of this book to learn how to get the FREE E- BOOK gift!

Remember to check your junk mail if you cannot find our email confirmation and subscribe for our FREE gifts and other promotions!

My FREE gift to you.... (no strings attached)

Grab Your Copy Now!

E - BOOK Title:

BOOSTING YOUR CONFIDENCE AND SELF-ESTEEM

OPEN LINK BELOW FOR INSTANT ACCESS

LINK:

http://eepurl.com/cWAvhj

www.ingramcontent.com/pod-product-compliance
Lightning Source LLC
Chambersburg PA
CBHW071132280526
45787CB00003B/1255